My Canadian Boyfriend,
JUSTIN TRUDEAU

—CARRIE PARKER—

My Canadian Boyfriend,
JUSTIN TRUDEAU

UNIVERSE

I have a new boyfriend. You haven't met him. He lives in Canada. His name is Justin Trudeau.

I first saw Justin in 2015 when my *Gilmore Girls* binge ended and the six o'clock news began. The anchors were reporting about the awful ugly things that were happening in the world. Then, after a series of commercials about the agonies of brittle bones, skin conditions, bowel blockages, and two-for-one buffet dinners (which may, according to the news reports just aired, result in brittle bones, skin conditions, and bowel blockages), Justin's shining face appeared, and my world completely changed.

Justin had just won some sort of national contest for adorableness or something. Thousands stood cheering him. I, too, rose to my feet, and as the crumbs of various salty-sweet snack foods fell from my lap, the weight of the world fell from my shoulders. I saw forever in his eyes. I saw happiness in his smile. I saw Future Me introducing him at brunch to my mother, who was just about to embarrass me by showing him photos of High School Me.

His compassion and kindness, not to mention his killer bod, make him the primest minister I've ever seen. With Justin right across the border, my nerves are calmed, my heart beats faster, and my fears become bête noires—because that sounds more French Canadian and, therefore, nicer.

Justin Trudeau is my Canadian boyfriend, and my love for him is real.

My boyfriend's kind of a big deal.

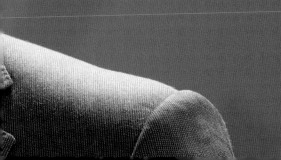

My boyfriend has a pretty busy schedule,
but I follow him on social media.

My boyfriend has been putting the "prime" in "Prime Minister" since 2015.

I'm not much of a beer drinker, but
I do enjoy a tall cool glass of Canadian water.

My boyfriend sometimes gazes northward,
far passed the snowy plains of Nunavut,
and smiles, knowing that the future he sees
is indeed female.

Yippe-Ki-Yay!

O, Canada!

Sometimes my silly boyfriend "poutines" in public.

J'apprends le francais parce que Justin est mon petit ami canadien que tu n'as pas encore recontre et il parle francais et j'amie beacoup manger des frites et faire du pain et boire du vin surtout avec lui.*

* Merci to Monsieur le Google Translate™ for his assistance.

Just when my boyfriend couldn't get any cuter, he holds a baby.

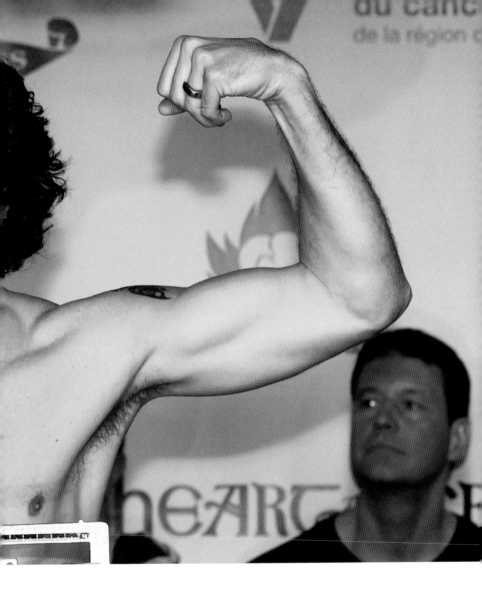

My boyfriend is quite the knockout.

What a good boy.

My boyfriend has a super busy schedule, but he finds time to hang with the bros when it's important . . .

. . . or when there's a game on!

My boyfriend appreciates a woman
who persists.

My boyfriend's outdoorsy.

My boyfriend is perfect for day or evening.

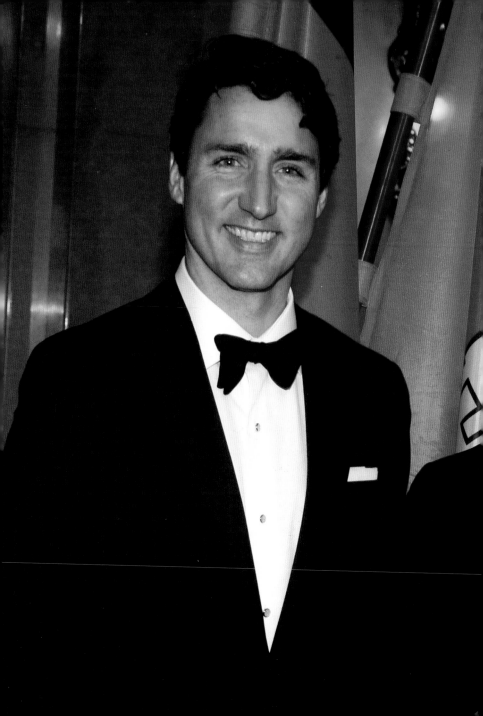

My boyfriend treats every woman like a queen.

My boyfriend has my whole heart in his hands.

My boyfriend is a skilled orator.

My boyfriend is the perfect accessory to
any outfit.

My boyfriend has the perfect balance of confidence, compassion, and swagger.

The Vancouver
Board of Trade

My boyfriend is an active listener.

The Vancouver
Board of Trade

I know women need to support each other,
but . . . c'mon.

#mycanadianboyfriend

Thanks, Bono, I found what I'm looking for!

My boyfriend says "love is not a crime,"
but his smile is a a killer!

My boyfriend understands the difference between celebrating diversity and cultural appropriation.

Run, Justin! Run the government! Run!

I'm not a spiritual person but my boyfriend's eyebrows are my patronus.

My boyfriend is everyone's moment of zen.

Justin says he was raised with a pretty thick skin, but it's clear that he also uses a really good moisturizer.

Find someone who looks at you like
Kate looks at my boyfriend.

Canada Day may technically be July 1,
but I see fireworks whenever I Google
"Justin Trudeau."
Which is every day.

My boyfriend's the kind of man who is unafraid to take matters into his own hands.

TFW you're checking out more than books.

My boyfriend is dreamy.

My boyfriend's sock game is always on point.

Seriously. Always.

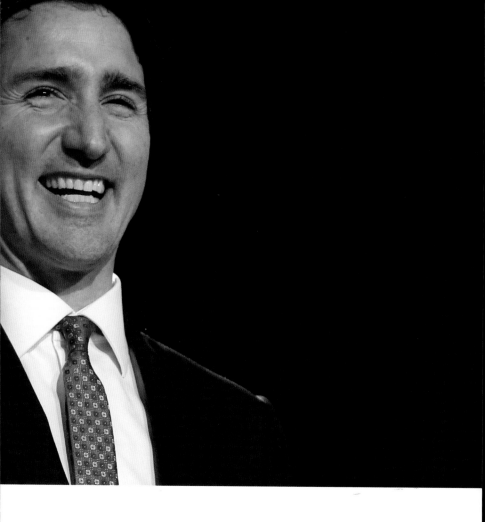

My boyfriend gives me the warm and fuzzies.

Classic Justin!

Justin once said "People think that boxing is all about how hard you can hit your opponent. It's not. Boxing is about how hard a hit you can take and keep going." I think it's also about him in those adorable shorts.

The thirst is real.

My boyfriend can make any setting look better.

My boyfriend knows every Celine Dion and
Leonard Cohen karaoke song.

People talk about how cold Canada can be,
but it looks pretty hot to me.

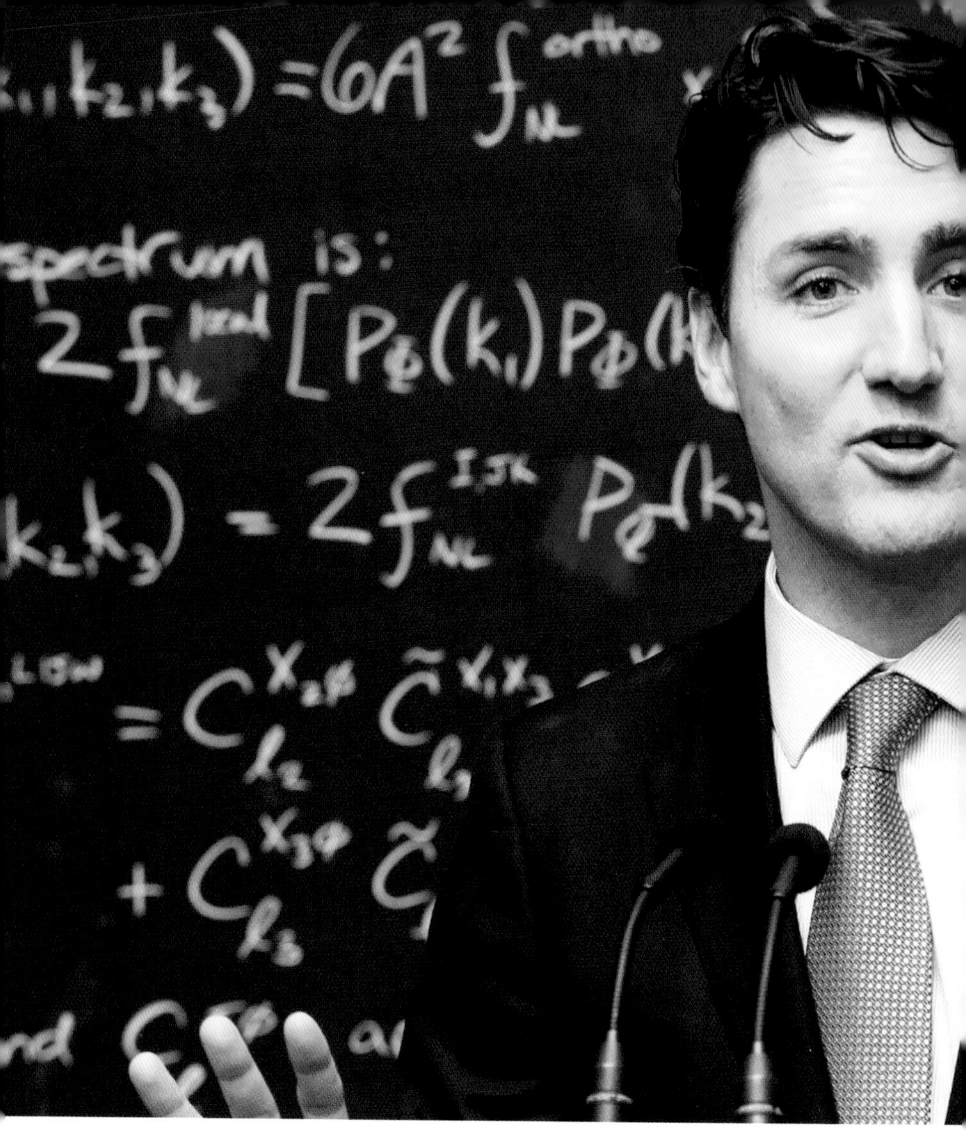

Talk nerdy to me, Justin!

My boyfriend loves giving high-fives!

. . . to everyone!

My boyfriend makes the wheels on my bus go round and round.

My boyfriend is a BBQtiepie.

Thanks, Mrs. Trudeau!
Or can I call you "Mom?"

My boyfriend thinks before he writes.
Or emails. Or Tweets.

Is it hot in here
or is it just
my boyfriend's
degrees?

My boyfriend likes a good landing strip.

My boyfriend: The Northern Star.

My boyfriend projects confidence.

Though he may not agree with his opponents, my boyfriend always tries to see all sides of debate.

My boyfriend knows when to drop the mic.

My boyfriend's name is Trudeau.
Justin Trudeau.

With very special thanks to Jessica Fuller, Charles Miers, Celina Carvalho, Susan Lynch, Nichole Beaulieu, Jono Jarrett, Laura Wannamaker, Victoria Daus, Emily Folks, and Wendy Nyemaster for their support of my completely rational, totally not-stalkery relationship goals; to the great and good people of Canada for their impeccable taste in politicians; to Sophie Gregorie Trudeau for sharing her husband with the world; and, of course, to my boyfriend, Justin Trudeau, for obvious reasons.

PHOTO CREDITS

Anadolu Agency (pp. 10–11); The Asahi Shimbun/Getty Images (pp. 122–23); Shaun Best/Reuters Pictures (p. 43); Mark Blinch/Reuters Pictures (pp. 11); Bloomberg/Getty Images (pp. 2–3); Remo Casilli/Reuters Pictures (pp. 124–25); Mike Cassese/Reuters Pictures (pp. 64–65); Noel Celis/Getty Images (pp. 114–15); Andy Clark/Reuters Pictures (pp. 26–27); dpa picture alliance/Alamy Stock Photo (pp. 6–7, 76–77, 90–91, 108–09); Frederick Florin/Getty Images (pp. 116–17); Samir Hussein/Getty Images (p. 127); Chris Jackson/Getty Images (pp. 30–31); Todd Korol/Reuters Pictures (pp. 16, 36); Rick Madonik/Getty Images (pp. 98–99); MediaPunch, Inc. (pp. 5, 67); © Copyright Jocelyn Michel/ leconsulat.ca (cover, pp. 40–41); Christine Muschi/Reuters Pictures (pp. 20–21, 46–47, 54–55, 100–01); Roberto Machado Noa/Getty Images (pp. 104–05); Lucas Oleniuk/Getty Images (pp. 17, 74–75); Carlos Osorio/Getty Images (pp. 102–03); PA Images/Alamy Stock Photo (pp. 28–29, 38–39, 44–45, 120–21); Guadalupe Pardo/Reuters Pictures (pp. 88–89); Performance Image/Alamy Stock Photo (pp. 12–13); Pool/Getty Images (p. 112–13); Pool/Reuters Pictures (p. 23); Reuters (pp. 34–35); Mark Spowart/Alamy Stock Photo (pp. 14–15, 92–93); Vince Talotta/Getty Images (pp. 94–95); The Canadian Press/Nathan Denette (pp. 96–97); The Canadian Press/Ryan Remiorz (pp. 80–81); The Canadian Press/Adrian Wyld (p. 106); Torontonian/Alamy Stock Photo (pp. 118–19); Chris Wattie/Reuters Pictures (pp. 8–9, 18–19, 24–25, 32–33, 50–51, 60–61, 70–71, 73, 78–79, 82–87, back cover); WENN Ltd./Alamy Stock Photo (pp. 36, 68–69); Xinhua/Alamy Stock Photo (pp. 52–53, 58–59); ZUMA Press, Inc./Alamy Stock Photo (pp. 48–49, 56, 62–63).

My boyfriend is so self confident
he doesn't need to take all the credit.

First published in the United States of America in 2018 by
Universe Publishing, a division of
Rizzoli International Publications, Inc.
300 Park Avenue South
New York, NY 10010
www.rizzoliusa.com

2018 2019 2020 2021 2022 / 10 9 8 7 6 5 4 3 2 1

Printed in China

Designer: Celina Carvalho

ISBN-13: 978-0-7893-3428-2
Library of Congress Control Number: 2017951960